Original title:
The Palm's Whisper

Copyright © 2025 Creative Arts Management OÜ
All rights reserved.

Author: Robert Ashford
ISBN HARDBACK: 978-1-80581-666-9
ISBN PAPERBACK: 978-1-80581-193-0
ISBN EBOOK: 978-1-80581-666-9

Reflections from a Hidden Grove

In a grove where shadows play,
A squirrel danced the night away.
He wore a hat made of bright leaves,
And giggled at the tricks he weaves.

A bird sang songs of silly things,
While teasing frogs with floppy wings.
They leaped around in wild ballet,
Creating laughter in the fray.

A breeze came by, did quite a twirl,
Chased a gopher, gave him a whirl.
With every swerve, the jokes would thrive,
In this place, all felt so alive.

Now daisies chuckle, and trees smile wide,
As laughter echoes, like a joyous tide.
In the grove where fun won't cease,
Nature's jesters find their peace.

Gentle Breaths of the Tropics

In breezy hats, we dance and twirl,
With mango slices, our laughter's pearl.
Old coconuts, they start to lose,
Their weight in jokes and silly snooze.

A parrot jokes while stealing chips,
It's all in fun, but watch those quips!
Swaying low, the palm trees grin,
As tourists strut with sunburned skin.

Flesh of the Warm Earth

On sun-soaked shores, we lay like blobs,
    Chasing crabs and dodging mobs.
    Flip-flops flying, oh what a sight,
    As we attempt a beachside flight!

    Grilling fish with laughter loud,
    Our jokes somehow attract a crowd.
    Belly flops are a work of art,
Though not quite what we call the heart.

Sighs of the Tropical Twilight

As fireflies paint the balmy night,
We roast marshmallows, oh what a sight!
Moonlight chuckles with a glow so sweet,
While we try the conga on our feet!

The stars give winks, like someone's teased,
The crickets chirp, as if they're pleased.
Sips of coconut, we share with glee,
And laugh at selfies, one, two, three!

Messages from the Lush Boughs

In the orchard, secrets float on high,
Trees gossip low, oh my, oh my!
Bananas giggle with a wink,
While the avocados start to think.

A squirrel's tale of the nut it lost,
Had all the branches laughing, engrossed.
Leaves dance wildly in a weaving spree,
As we gobble fruit and shout with glee!

Messages on the Gentle Breeze

A breeze comes by with tales to share,
Of dancing socks on the neighbor's chair.
It tickles noses, makes dogs sneeze,
And whispers secrets from the trees.

Leaves chuckle softly, a giggle spread,
As squirrels argue who gets the bread.
"Not mine!" they shout, with a playful leap,
Breezy messages, laughter they keep.

Enchanted by the Leaves' Language

Leaves rustle like a gossip crew,
Talking about a cat that flew.
Amidst the branches, jokes they weave,
Each one grinning, I can believe!

A breeze picks up, the laughter swells,
As one leaf starts its stand-up spells.
"Why did the tree start telling jokes?
To branch out more," it surely pokes!

Sails of the Tranquil Waters

On calm waters, ducks have a chat,
With a quack and a flap about this and that.
They sail on by, with hats askew,
"Oy, look at me!" quips one in a shoe!

Reflections ripple, giggles abound,
As fish swim past, with laughter profound.
"Swim faster, mate, don't break your fins!
Or we'll lose our game of water spins!"

Ode to the Green Adornments

Oh, verdant hats on heads so bold,
With flowers peeking out, the stories told.
A plant decides it's time to dance,
While wearing leaves, it takes a chance!

Grass growing high, gets tickled pink,
And whispers tales over the brink.
"Look at my style," it gives a twirl,
As daisies chuckle, giving a whirl!

Murmurs of the Island's Heart

Beneath the swaying trees so tall,
A coconut drops with a comic call.
The crabs scuttle with claws in the air,
As if they're dancing without a care.

Seagulls squawk, they gossip in flight,
While turtles play hide-and-seek at night.
A parrot's joke, colorful and loud,
Makes even the shyest fish feel proud.

Dance of the Green Sentinels

Leaves giggle in the playful breeze,
As vines twist 'round with the greatest of ease.
A chameleon shows off its crazy flair,
Turning bright orange and then back to air.

The lizards laugh in the afternoon sun,
Feeling quite grand in their mini run.
With each flip and twist, all the creatures grin,
There's mischief abounding — let the fun begin!

Secrets Carried on Gentle Winds

Whispers float on the breeze's back,
A sea turtle's tales of a snail attack!
Island mice plan their midnight feast,
Where cheese is the goal and fun's the beast.

Flip-flops collide, it sounds like a band,
As friends chase each other across the sand.
With laughter so bright on this lively shore,
The secrets of joy are what we adore!

Lullabies from the Sunlit Oasis

In a hammock swing, the frogs croak a tune,
Inviting the fireflies under the moon.
Dreamy palms sway and giggle away,
As night tickles laughter from day to day.

The stars join in with a twinkling jest,
As the moonlight hosts its very own fest.
Sleepy sloths drift with smiles on their face,
In this oasis of fun, we find our place.

Alchemy of Light and Leaf

In the forest, beams of light,
Tickle leaves as they take flight.
Squirrels giggle, chase the rays,
Dancing in their cheeky ways.

Frogs croak jokes beneath the trees,
Mixing laughter with the breeze.
Sunlight's potion, bright and clear,
Turns each shadow into cheer.

Rabbits wear their funny hats,
Competing with the cheeky rats.
In this tale of glowing fun,
Every leaf's a joke begun.

As the sun begins to fade,
Laughter trails that light has made.
The forest hums a joyful song,
In this place, we all belong.

Nightfall's Embrace in the Jungle

As the sun dips low and sly,
Monkeys swing and shout, oh my!
Fireflies flash a dance of glee,
While owls hoot, "Come laugh with me!"

Bananas wear their peels askew,
Chasing shadows, just for you.
Lizards laugh in sneaky leaps,
Jumping high, but who still sleeps?

Bats with capes offer a show,
Encouraging the jungle's flow.
Every vine a tickling chase,
In this wild and quirky place.

The night unfolds, it giggles loud,
Wrapping critters in its shroud.
In the dark, it's clear to see,
Laughter found in mystery.

Echoes of Green Fronds

In the rustle of the leaves,
Whispers travel, like old thieves.
Each frond tells a different tale,
Of squirrels plotting their next fail.

Cicadas giggle, sing their song,
As the green gets wild and strong.
In the shade, the shadows play,
Daring pranks throughout the day.

Daisies giggle, grass does sway,
As the breeze joins in the fray.
Peeking flowers try to tease,
Every passerby with ease.

In echoing laughs, the forest beams,
Where humor flows like bubbling streams.
Nature's jesters, if you see,
These green fronds laugh light-heartedly.

Secrets of Sunlit Shadows

When the sun begins to rise,
Shadows dance, oh what a surprise!
Dancing figures waltzing free,
In the light, they sing with glee.

Leaves murmur secrets, oh so sly,
As the breeze whispers, "Why not try?"
The ground's alive with teasing roots,
Singing songs in playful boots.

Daffodils join in the jest,
Making sure they look their best.
When sunlight hits, they start to sway,
Turning shadows into play.

In this land of light and cheer,
Every shadow brings a sneer.
What a joy when rays abound,
In sunlit secrets, laughter's found.

Harmonies of Nature's Retreat

In the forest, a squirrel prances,
He's planning a nutty dance in chances.
The birds all pause, perched on a line,
They critique his moves, oh so divine!

A raccoon rolls, with mischief in eyes,
He's stealing snacks, oh what a surprise!
The trees are giggling, leaves shaking loose,
As they whisper secrets, of what's profuse.

The river chuckles, a bubbly flow,
Tickling the stones with a gentle glow.
Frogs join the chorus, croaking in glee,
Nature's comedy, wild as can be.

A chameleon laughs, changing his hue,
While a butterfly flirts, it's all in the view.
In this retreat, the laughter resounds,
Nature's hilarity endlessly abounds.

Fables of the Silent Grove

In a grove where the statuesque trees stand proud,
The owls tell jokes, their voices loud.
A laugh shakes the branches, rustling the leaves,
As absurdity dances, the grove believes.

A turtle cracks jokes, his pace slow but sly,
While the rabbits are laughing, oh my, oh my!
The fables unfold, with giggles galore,
In this silent grove, humor's at the core.

The fox shares tales, with whimsical flair,
Of adventures gone wrong, it's a hilarious affair.
The mushrooms are chuckling with caps in a twist,
As nature's comedians create a funny mist.

In the silent grove where the wit takes a bow,
Even the tranquil brook can't help but allow,
For laughter to flow like a bubbling stream,
Where every creature fulfills a dream.

Breath of the Whispering Islands

On islands where the palm trees sway and shake,
A parrot quips jokes, for goodness' sake!
With each playful squawk, the island erupts,
In fits of laughter, all worries disrupted.

The sand crabs are dancing, clumsy and spry,
With shells as their costumes, oh my, oh my!
The tide rolls in giggling, water like foam,
In this laughter-rich land, all find a home.

A turtle takes selfies, with a wink and a smile,
While the seagulls critique him from up high for a while.
The coconut drinks cheers, clinking away,
In this cheerful paradise, humor holds sway.

The sun sets in colors, a canvas so bright,
As the day turns to night, laughter takes flight.
With every soft breeze, a chuckle does glide,
The spirit of joy, forever will bide.

Shadows of the Gentle Dancer

In twilight's embrace, the shadows start to play,
A mouse tricks a cat, in a comical way.
With twirls and leaps, the fireflies glow,
As laughter ignites in the soft evening flow.

The raccoon, a dancer with mischief galore,
Hosts a moonlit gala, oh what a score!
Every critter invites, with curious cheer,
As they jig and they jive, their worries disappear.

The owls watch closely, with wise, twinkling eyes,
They hoot out advice, wrapped in surprise.
From the ground to the sky, the hairs on the neck,
All tremble with laughter, in this silly speck.

With footfalls of joy, until morning's light,
In shadows of dancers, all loses the fight.
For humor takes flight in this whimsical chance,
As the night wears away, through laughter we prance.

Dance of the Fragrant Foliage

Leaves sway gently, what a sight,
They boogie best when there's sunlight.
Breeze joins in with a nimble jig,
While squirrels prance, oh, what a gig!

A chipmunk croons, pulling a face,
To every beat, it keeps the pace.
Laughter echoes in the branches,
As branches sway, they take their chances.

Petals twirl like they're out for a spin,
While ants march in, determined to win.
With every rustle, a chuckle shared,
Nature's bash, completely unprepared.

In the midst of this leafy ball,
A grasshopper leaps, then takes a fall.
With twinkling eyes and fruits on display,
The fragrant woods just dance all day!

Murmurs of a Sun-Kissed Grove

In a grove where sunshine beams,
Trees gossip softly in golden dreams.
They chitter-chatter, what a crew,
Silly jokes just drift on through.

A rabbit hops, with ears on high,
Joining in, oh me, oh my!
With every rustle, giggles rise,
Who knew trees could be so wise?

Twigs snap, and an owl hoots back,
"Who's cracking up? Now that's a fact!"
Leaves tickle each other in jest,
Nature's hub, it's an endless fest.

With all this fun, you may well find,
The sun-kissed grove is quite unrefined.
A place where laughter takes its flight,
And all are merry, from day to night!

Silhouettes in the Twilight Canopy

Twilight paints the sky with glee,
Shadows stretch, now look and see!
A raccoon prances, strutting with pride,
In evening's glow, it cannot hide.

Fireflies blink, a dance so bright,
While owls chuckle at the sight.
"Who knew nights could bring such fun?"
The moon giggles, "Oh, I'm the one!"

Branches sway, creating a show,
As night gives way, a softer glow.
Buds whisper secrets, wild and free,
While crickets chirp, "Join in with me!"

In this twilight, laughter soars,
Nature's mischief, it never bores.
With each silhouette and playful spark,
The canopy glows bright in the dark!

Secrets Breathed by Nature

In every rustle, tales take flight,
Whispers giggle in the moonlight.
A breeze recounts with airy might,
Nature's secrets, kept with delight.

Bumblebees buzz with cheeky flair,
"Did you hear? They think we care!"
With nectar sweet, they claim their ground,
As flowers laugh, a joyful sound.

A wise old tree, with bark so thick,
Shares a joke about a stubborn stick.
"Why didn't he move? He was so rooted!
Couldn't leave, so he just booted!"

Every leaf, a tale to tell,
Of rainy days and sunny spells.
In this world where laughter sways,
Nature's secrets fill our days!

Embrace of Tropical Breezes

In the shade where guavas fall,
A lazy lizard takes a crawl.
The sun's too hot, the breeze is nice,
He dreams of ice cream and some rice.

Coconuts are known to drop,
And give the locals quite a pop.
They laugh and run, trying to dodge,
While sipping punch, oh what a smudge!

At dusk, the fireflies play their tricks,
Dancing wildly, doing flips.
A parrot squawks a cheeky tune,
As tourists giggle under the moon.

So here we'll bask in sunny fun,
With laughs that burst like bubbles spun.
In breezy gi, we'll sway and twirl,
Life's a laugh in this tropical whirl!

Serenade of the Swaying Leaves

The leaves dance like they stole a beat,
While ants march proudly on their feet.
A breeze whispers secrets in the trees,
Dropping acorns like confetti with ease.

Swaying branches hold a choir,
As birds mix tunes that never tire.
A monkey swings with a cheeky grin,
Called to perform but forgot to begin.

Hummingbirds hover, just for fun,
While squirrels plot how to steal a bun.
In this concert under the skies,
Every giggle is a sweet surprise.

With laughter shared high above,
The breezes carry tales of love.
In this land where joy won't cease,
Every rustle is a chance for peace.

Lullabies Beneath the Canopy

Under the canopy, shadows play,
With critters chatting their own way.
A frog croaks loudly, claiming big fame,
While crickets laugh, their response is lame.

A sloth hugs branches, moving so slow,
Dreaming of a burrito made to-go.
Twirling leaves get caught in the fray,
As the sun dips low, fading to gray.

The breezes hum a gentle tune,
While fireflies sparkle like tiny balloons.
A raccoon sneezes, oh what a sound!
Echoing laughter all around.

So snuggle tight in nature's lap,
Where each silly noise is a joyful clap.
In this happy spot, we find our bliss,
With giggles shared in the woods' sweet kiss.

Whispers on the Ocean Breeze

On the shore where seabirds squawk,
A clumsy crab takes a little walk.
He slips and slides right in the sand,
As kids all giggle and form a band.

Waves come crashing, oh what a splash,
A sandcastle's fate—a sudden crash!
With moans of laughter rolling wide,
As seashells giggle, hiding inside.

The wind brings tales from afar,
Of fishy dramas and a fallen star.
With salty snacks and drinks in hand,
We savor jokes and sandy sand.

So gather round, let laughter unfurl,
In this seaside retreat, life's a whirl.
With whispers soft and joys that tease,
We find our fun in the ocean breeze.

Vibrations of the Island Symphony

Bamboo flutes play tunes so neat,
While coconuts dance to the beat.
Crabs tap shoes with a clumsy flair,
Underneath the sun's warm glare.

Seagulls squawk in silly rounds,
Twirling round like circus clowns.
Tropical birds wear hats so bright,
Singing softly into the night.

Waves clap hands and join the show,
As driftwood surfer poses grow.
Fish giggle as they jump and twirl,
Splashing water with a joyful swirl.

So join the fun, don't miss a sound,
On this quirky, lively ground.
Where laughter rolls like tides so free,
In this symphony by the sea.

Songs of the Waving Blossoms

Blossoms waltz in breezy cheer,
Teaching bees to dance so near.
Hummingbirds in bowties bright,
Twirl and flit, a funny sight!

Lilies giggle at the breeze,
Spreading tales with such great ease.
Petals whisper silly dreams,
Underneath the sun's bright beams.

Daisies wear their crowns askew,
Pansies laugh, say, 'Join us too!'
In this garden, joy's the key,
As flowers sing in harmony.

So frolic 'neath this vibrant space,
Where blooms and laughter interlace.
Every blossom holds a tune,
Dancing under the cheeky moon.

Language of the Dancing Woods

Trees twist funny, roots in knots,
Squirrels giggle in silly spots.
Leaves shimmy, rustle to the beat,
While chipmunks tap with little feet.

Branches whisper jokes so dry,
As owls hoot with a wink and sly.
Wisps of vines play peekaboo,
Making shadows dance for you.

Frogs croak tunes of pure delight,
Making every critter's night.
Mice pull pranks like seasoned pros,
Where laughter in the forest flows.

So come and join this wooded cheer,
Where every creature yells, "I'm here!"
In the woods of giggles and wise,
Nature's humor never lies.

Memories in the Shade of Green

In the shade, the breezes tease,
Leaves chuckle, dancing with ease.
Picnics full of laughter and fun,
As ants march in a funny run.

Squirrels share their nutty tales,
While turtles race like tiny snails.
Sunbeams twinkle through the trees,
Creating shadows just to please.

Kites soar high with giggles loud,
As kids tumble, proud and unbowed.
In this green space, joy's a stream,
Where every moment's like a dream.

Let's weave memories, wild and bright,
In the shade, where everything's right.
Laugh together, let spirits soar,
In this haven, we'll dance once more.

The Language of Falling Fronds

Fronds hang low, they start to sway,
Whispering secrets, come what may.
Dance like a clown, with style so bright,
Trees chuckle softly, 'What a sight!'

The sun peeks in, with a cheeky grin,
Fronds gossip lightly, let the games begin.
One turns a twirl, then trips on a shoe,
The grass erupts, laughing like it knew.

With a rustle and a shake, they start to tease,
'Hey, look at us, we're catching the breeze!'
An acorn joins in, a goofy old chap,
Rolling down the path, taking a nap.

In the breeze, a comedy plays,
As fronds toss jokes in the sun's warm rays.
With every flutter, a giggle they share,
Nature's own stand-up, if you dare!

Glimmers of Hidden Landscapes

Underneath canopies, the shadows all dance,
Glimmers of laughter, nature's romance.
A squirrel in shades, sipping on tea,
Winks at the fronds, 'Come chill with me!'

The breeze blows softly, tickling the trees,
Leaves rustle secrets, caught in the breeze.
A feather floats down, a critic so fine,
Whispering truths, 'This humor's divine!'

Caterpillars giggle at the birds overhead,
'You think you can soar? We'll munch instead!'
The ground shakes with laughter, a right old shindig,
Every creature here joins in, small and big.

With beams of sunlight, laughter ignites,
In these hidden realms, fun takes flight.
Every twist in nature holds a punchline,
With giggles galore, all perfectly fine!

Journey of an Autumn Leaf

An autumn leaf flutters, a ship in the air,
Waving goodbye, with a flamboyant flair.
It sails through the sky, wearing a grin,
'Time for adventure, let chaos begin!'

Spinning and twirling, a dance on its way,
Bumping the branches, in glorious play.
'Hey there, flower! A little respect?'
But the daisies just giggle, 'We stand direct!'

A gust of wind offers a comical ride,
The leaf turns and twists, full of pride.
'Look at me go! I'm the king of this street!'
As the ground yells back, 'Now that's quite a feat!'

Landing with flair on a pile of its kin,
The leaf laughs aloud, at this fun little spin.
Together they chuckle, in autumn's bright glow,
What a wild journey, putting on quite the show!

Nishan of the Breezy Glade

In the glade so lovely, the breezes do play,
Fronds and flowers join in a merry ballet.
Dandelions giggle, blowing out wishes,
While crickets perform with their chirpy swishes!

A frog in a bowtie croaks out a joke,
'Why did the leaf avoid that bloke?'
The flowers all titter, 'We're all ears!'
As they sway with laughter, dissolving their fears.

Butterflies prance, with vestments so bright,
Flattering fronds in the dappled light.
Together they spin, nature's good cheer,
In the breezy glade, there's nothing to fear!

As day turns to dusk, the laughter goes on,
A night full of whimsy, a magical dawn.
In the heart of the glade, where fun knows no bounds,
Nature rolls over, with mirthful sounds!

Tides of Green in the Breeze

In the garden, plants start to sway,
Chasing butterflies, what a play!
Lively leaves in a rooty dance,
They giggle loud, given half a chance.

A tomato whispers, 'I'm just shy!'
While radishes yell, 'Don't ask us why!'
In this patch, a rumor spreads,
'Carrots are hiding beneath their beds!'

Sunflowers nod in the warm sun's glow,
"Can you believe we once were just seeds, though?"
A bee makes a joke that flies right by,
Laughing aloud, "Where'd my left wing guy?"

Clovers laugh under the moon's winks,
"Mice play cards while the garden drinks!"
Nature's pranks, in every leaf and bend,
Who knew that greens could joyfully pretend?

Serenade of the Verdant Guardians

In the woods, the trees pull faces,
Swapping stories in leafy braces.
A squirrel giggles, tail all a-fluff,
"Who can spot the acorn? It's tough!"

An owl hoots out a pun so wise,
"Don't leaf too soon, or miss the surprise!"
Moss giggles softly, in hues of jade,
"I'm the softest seat you've ever made!"

The ferns do a dance, all twirl and twine,
"Watch us shimmy like grapes on a vine!"
A brook babbles jokes, splashing with glee,
"Try to catch me, you'll need more than three!"

Brambles chuckle, in a tangle of snickers,
"Why did the soil start doing kickers?"
Roots share a laugh at how small they seem,
In this forest, everybody's got a dream!

Mysteries in the Ocean's Embrace

Beneath the waves, fish know a tune,
"Did you hear the crab? He hums to the moon!"
An octopus winks, his colors a blaze,
"Is that a fish or just a great phase?"

A dolphin darts, full of silly flair,
"Why do we swim? We just love the air!"
Starfish giggle at the tales they spin,
"Caught a great wave, like a whimsy twin!"

Seahorses lounge, sipping seaweed tea,
"Who wore it better, let's wait and see!"
The coral reef hosts a fishy parade,
"Guess who forgot and swam in the shade?"

A turtle grins, as slow as can be,
"Life's but a race, let it glide with glee!"
In ocean depths, where laughter unfurls,
Mysteries swim, and joy swirls and whirls!

Heartbeats Amidst the Canopy

Above the ground, the branches chatter,
"Why do we flutter? To make hearts shatter!"
A parrot squawks in a flamboyant hue,
"Who wore it better? Me or the dew?"

Squirrels leap with acorn delight,
"Yesterday's stash is hidden from sight!"
Long limbs stretch, a comedy show,
"Why can't trees play cards? They're too slow!"

Vines twist playfully, heroes in frames,
"Do you know why the frogs made names?"
The forest hums with a giggling breeze,
Invisible friendships sway through the leaves.

In every shadow where sunlight teases,
Nature's jesters bring laughter and breezes.
With every heartbeat, the forest's a clown,
In the canopy's arms, fun and joy abound!

Veils of Verdant Serenity

In leafy hats where squirrels scheme,
They play hide and seek, or so it seems.
A bug rolls by in a tiny car,
Laughing, he says, "I'm off to the bar!"

The branches sway in a breezy dance,
As birds gossip on their chance romance.
With each soft rustle, a ticklish plea,
"Come join us here, oh what glee!"

Moss-covered rocks wear party shoes,
While rabbits jest in colorful hues.
Each giggle shakes the very leaves,
Nature's jesters, in fun, they weave!

With sunshine spilling creamy light,
Pine-cones roll off in a playful flight.
Oh, who knew nature could be so grand?
Bringing joy with a leafy hand!

Hushed Stories in the Shade

Underneath a leafy crown,
Two frogs gossip without a frown.
"Did you see the cat's latest leap?"
"Quite a sight, I could not sleep!"

The shadows wink and stretch their arms,
As ants march on, in friendly charms.
A sleepy tortoise joins the chat,
"Why hurry, friends? I'm far from that!"

A breeze tickles the tales they weave,
While bees buzz by, oh how they cleave!
In this shade, laughter takes its form,
Life's funnies swirl, a joyful storm!

Where sunbeams slip through the leaves' art,
The earth smiles, cradling each heart.
Here, under shade, we all can play,
What's the fuss? Let's joke away!

Rhythm of the Serene Leaves

Leaves tap dance, what a sight to see,
While crickets chirp in harmony.
Even the flowers join the groove,
Making sure they find their move!

Breezes tickle, the branches sing,
Dancing together like a spring fling.
The lizards strike poses, oh so bold,
In this leafy world, stories unfold!

A sleepy owl hoots out a jest,
"Why don't trees ever get a rest?"
They laugh till dusk covers the day,
In the rhythm of life, who can stray?

Oh, the joy in each leaf's spin,
Nature's party, let's dive in!
Here, fun lives on with vibrant flair,
Where the green twirls end and laughter's air!

Whispers from the Coastal Haven

Waves giggle softly, tickle the shore,
While seagulls squawk of riches galore.
A crab tiptoes, trying to boast,
"I've got the best shell, I'm such a host!"

Sunbathers laugh, covered in sand,
With grumpy fish, trying to find land.
"Mmm, do I swim or shall I sun?"
"Just flip a coin; it's all in fun!"

Caught in a net of silly tales,
The jellyfish dance through ocean trails.
Each wave a wink, each breeze a cheer,
Funny whispers fill the air here!

As sunsets blush and day takes flight,
Nature's humor shines so bright.
From the coastal lines to the azure skies,
Laughter rolls in with the tide's sweet sighs!

Phrases from the Sun-Kissed Grove

In the grove where laughter flies,
Every tree wears a funny disguise.
A squirrel jokes with the sun's bright ray,
While birds chirp puns throughout the day.

Beneath the leaves, a light breeze chuckles,
Crickets dance with joyful huddles.
A lizard slips on a sunlit track,
Waving 'hi' and never looking back.

The flowers giggle, their petals sway,
Each bloom throws shade in a playful way.
Butterflies flutter, their colors blink,
As they join in the grove's cheeky wink.

So come and join this vibrant spree,
Where every giggle is wild and free.
In the grove of humor, we'll laugh and roam,
Finding joy in every leafy home.

Breaths of the Verdant Whisperers

In leafy tales where shadows play,
Lush greens speak with a funny sway.
The breeze cracks jokes that tickle the air,
While blossoms blush with laughter to share.

A toad croaks wise with a comical tune,
As butterflies bring laughter at noon.
Grasshoppers hop with a wink and a jig,
Making the world feel just a bit big.

Sunbeams dance on a dewy leaf,
Winking at clouds in humorous belief.
Every gust of wind a playful tease,
With secrets shared among the trees.

So linger here, where the laughter flows,
With every whisper, the fun just grows.
In this vibrant world, let's twirl and cheer,
Finding joy in every fleeting year.

Dreams Cradled by Sunny Leaves

In the canopy, dreams have fun,
Twirling under the melting sun.
A raccoon grins with mischief delight,
As shadows giggle with sheer delight.

Bees buzz jokes in their busy flight,
While daisies sway in pure delight.
The sky winks down with a cloud's silly face,
Reminding us life is a playful race.

Underneath arches of sun-dappled green,
Every critter is a jester unseen.
In drizzles of giggles, laughter spills,
As the world spins in joyful thrills.

So let's bask in this dreamlike scene,
Where frolicsome thoughts are never routine.
With every leaf, there's a punchline near,
In a world full of fun, let's disappear.

Poem of the Whispering Wilderness

In the wild where whispers play,
Trees tell tales in a funny way.
A fox cracks puns with a tailored grin,
As owls hoot laughter, it's always a win.

The brook babbles secrets with bubbly cheer,
While frogs plop down, making it clear.
That life's a jest in this blooming ground,
With nature's chuckles all around.

Leaves rustle like giggling friends,
As sunlight dances, the laughter never ends.
A curious bear gives a playful roar,
Poking fun at the squirrels that soar.

So step into this wilderness bright,
Where humor takes flight in the blushing light.
In the arms of nature, let's laugh and roam,
Finding endless joy and a place called home.

Underneath the Leafy Veil

A squirrel with a nut so grand,
Winks at me; I wave my hand.
He gestures back, then takes a leap,
To hide the treasure in a heap.

I ask him where his stash will go,
He shrugs and grins, "I run the show!"
With leafy cap and tiny glee,
He's off with snacks, and still like me!

The leaves just giggle, rustling loud,
As if they're part of some nutty crowd.
I sit and chuckle, sipping tea,
While nature's jesters dance with glee.

So if you find your joy is low,
Just look for squirrels and let it flow.
With every leap and playful fall,
You'll find a laugh, you'll hear it all!

Twilight's Gentle Caress

At dusk, I spy a firefly's glow,
He winks at me, then steals the show.
I think he's got a honeyed plan,
To light the way for a tiny band.

But then a breeze! Oh, what a jest!
It tickles light, a gleeful quest.
The firefly spins, he takes a dive,
"Catch me!" he blinks—he's so alive!

A shadow sways with a laugh or two,
While crickets chirp their evening brew.
Twilight chuckles, down she crept,
As dreams of laughter slyly swept.

Oh, night, you're like a hat with flair,
With stars that twinkle here and there.
So gather 'round, friends, let's embrace,
The funny notes of this starry space!

Swaying Dreams Beneath the Sky

In breezy fields where grass is high,
The daisies swirl, they laugh, oh my!
A bumblebee with quite a plan,
Tries to tango—a wobbly man!

He bumps a flower, buzzes loud,
And makes the petals form a crowd.
They sway and giggle in delight,
As bumble dances through the night.

Clouds above play hide and seek,
Whispering secrets when they peek.
"Where's the sun?" asks a passing kite,
He chuckles, "Just give him a bite!"

Oh merry winds! Let laughter spread,
As flowers tease the sleepy bed.
In swaying dreams all worries fly,
With nature's jesters dancing by!

Ocean's Breath on a Quiet Evening

The waves roll in with a bubbly laugh,
They tickle my toes like a playful calf.
A crab in shades, all dressed to sway,
Struts along like it's a cabaret.

The seagulls squawk, a silly tune,
As they dance around under the moon.
They'll steal your fries, oh what a scene!
The ocean's jesters, a hungry team!

On sandy shores, the footprints write,
Of giggles shared 'til the stars ignite.
The tide pulls back with a cheeky grin,
"Come back soon, let the fun begin!"

So grab a shell and join the fun,
With ocean's breeze, we'll scamper run.
For in this laughter, spirits soar,
Life's a beach, let's laugh some more!

Threads of Verdant Whimsy

In a grove where green things dance,
Frogs wear hats, and bugs prance.
Leaves gossip, secrets they share,
While squirrels snicker without a care.

Twigs are wands for silly spells,
The grass hums tunes, oh, what yells!
Roots tickle toes, so watch your step,
Nature's jesters, a lighthearted prep.

A breeze tickles with a soft tease,
Dancing dandelions sway with ease.
Blades of grass play peek-a-boo,
Who knew green could be so blue?

The blooms are jesters, bright and bold,
Spinning tales that never get old.
With petals twirling, they take flight,
In this verdant realm of pure delight.

Journey Through the Leafy Labyrinth

Through leafy paths we twist and turn,
With each corner, new things to learn.
A raccoon giggles, a rabbit hops,
Chasing shadows—with funny plops.

The ferns are giants, we might get lost,
They're big and plush, but at what cost?
Silly signs point left, then right,
Can a tree wear a crown? What a sight!

We find a pond, where ducks wear ties,
Quacking laughably 'neath sunny skies.
Splashing with glee, they all agree,
Being silly is the best decree.

The maze wraps around, like a joke untold,
With silly pranks that never get old.
Roots high-five as we skip along,
In this leafy realm, we all belong.

Voiced in the Lush Stillness

In a grove where giggles flow,
Even mushrooms put on a show.
A babbling brook, with gurgling cheer,
Whispers secrets for all who hear.

A lizard struts, in shades of green,
Winks and grins, what a scene!
The sun sneezes, with rays so bright,
Turning shadows into a silly fright.

Caterpillars rock, as bugs applaud,
In this lush world, nature's a prod.
Grumpy trees grumble, but look, they smile,
A winding path turns into fun all the while.

The laughter echoes, soft and light,
In the stillness of day turns into night.
With critters chatting, the scene is set,
A lush encore, we'll never forget.

Nature's Quiet Monologue

Under the boughs, a whisper flows,
Where even the daisies crack silly jokes.
The crickets chirp in rhythmic sighs,
While chipmunks giggle at the size of pies.

The sun peeks in, with a playful grin,
As shadows dance, let the fun begin.
Acorns tumble, make a gentle sound,
Nature's jesters can always be found.

A slug slides by, taking its time,
It slides past daisies, plotting a rhyme.
With each little slip, it's a comedy show,
Who knew that slow could steal the flow?

So in this forest, where laughter's the song,
Nature's voice hums, playful and strong.
With every turn, a quirky tale,
Life's a romp on this leafy trail.

When the Shore Meets the Leaf

A leaf danced down, it took a dive,
The shore laughed loud, 'Guess we're alive!'
Waves tickled roots, so silly and sweet,
As sand made a throne for the wind's tiny feet.

Dunes yelled, 'Catch me! I'm piling high!'
Seagulls squawked, 'What a crazy sky!'
With every gust, the fun took flight,
A breezy ballet, oh what a sight!

Laughter echoed from tree to wave,
A rhythm of joy, oh how we crave!
In nature's jest, all worries cease,
The world is a stage, let's dance in peace!

So let the shore and the leaf collide,
In every giggle, let love abide.
For in this moment, so silly and grand,
We find our bliss in the playful sand.

Eulogy of the Swaying Silhouette

Oh, how they sway, those tall giants bold,
With stories of laughter, both new and old.
They nod at the breeze, gossiping low,
'Did you see that squirrel? Oh, how he'll show!'

Their shadows dance lightly across the ground,
Tickling the toes of all that surround.
'Watch your step!' the grass whispers with glee,
As petals take bets on who'll fall in free.

When the sun takes a bow, they shimmy in gold,
Each flutter a tale, so cheeky and bold.
'We sway for the giggles,' the silhouettes grin,
In the twilight, their laughter begins!

So gather 'round, friends, to join in the cheer,
For life's but a dance, let's shake off our fear.
The trees remind us, amidst all the strife,
To laugh and to sway, is the spirit of life.

Interlude in the Treetops

High up in the canopies, shouts of delight,
The branches all rumble, 'Who'll join the flight?'
A squirrel on a spy mission, tail feathers high,
Cracks jokes with the crows as they flutter by.

The owls roll their eyes, 'Not again with the puns,'
While rave parties happen with just the tree runs.
'Let's boogie!' they chirp, and swing to the beat,
A funky jam session, all nature on their feet!

With dappled light giggling through leafy screens,
A chorus of rustles sings sweetly between.
Who knew the high life was filled with such flair?
A waltz among branches, dance off your care!

So raise your juice cups to the treetop delight,
Where laughter and whimsy take glorious flight.
In this jolly paradise, joy's no disguise,
Join hands with the leaves, beneath endless skies!

Path of the Dreaming Canopy

Strolling beneath, where the dreamers sway,
Branches exchanging the secrets of play.
'Hey, leaf! Are you dizzy?' the stubborn roots laugh,
As they tug on the soil, their playful giraffe.

Beneath the green arches, the whispers conspire,
'Did you hear of the storm? It's a comic desire!'
But branches just giggle and dance with the breeze,
'Storms are just parties, with snacks from the trees!'

Wandering onward, let laughter unfold,
Every step on the path brings a story retold.
With sunlight as glitter, and shadows that sing,
Let's lose ourselves in the joy that they bring!

For in this grand journey, we frolic and leap,
Echoes of laughter, memories to keep.
So cherish each moment beneath the green dome,
In the dance of the dreaming, we all find a home!

Sagas of the Verdant Heart

In the jungle, leaves debate,
Who's the softest, who's more great?
A parrot squawks, a monkey swings,
While the ants just mock, and the critters sing.

Beneath the sun, they often jest,
Who makes the very best sun-drenched nest?
A lazy sloth, with style so clear,
Claims it's all about leisure, my dear!

The bamboo dances with a twist,
A squirrel teases, you can't resist.
Laughter echoes through the trees,
Even the flowers join with ease!

As dusk descends, tales are spun,
Of silly antics, just for fun.
The moonlight glows, a soft embrace,
In the verdant heart, they find their space.

Nature's Soft Confessions

The breeze carries whispers, oh so light,
About a beetle that took a flight.
With tiny goggles, it zooms around,
Chasing shadows, it's nature's clown!

A caterpillar, very chubby,
Dreams of wings, oh how it's stubby!
It wiggles and wriggles, wanting to fly,
But all it does is munch and sigh.

A turtle thinks it's a speedy car,
But takes its time, never goes far.
Giggling grasshoppers jump with glee,
While the tortoise cheers, "Hey, wait for me!"

At night's fall, stars giggle bright,
As creatures settle, it's quite a sight.
Nature laughs in a soft parade,
Where every joke is expertly made.

Secrets Hidden in the Breeze

The wind carries secrets, soft and sly,
Like a cheeky fox, it darts on by.
A flower blushes, in a flurry of pink,
Whispers a secret, and winks with a blink.

A kiwi bird, with its curious face,
Shuffles around at its own slow pace.
With a giggle it chirps, "Don't take me fast!"
"I'm on my own, let days be vast!"

Leaves rustle softly, sharing a joke,
Even the stones can't help but poke.
Through twilight's glow, laughter ensues,
Nature's gathering, with nothing to lose.

In the cool of the night, buzzes a bee,
Dancing with stars, so full of glee.
Secrets paint the air, a mischievous tease,
Hidden stories swirl, carried by the breeze.

Timeless Stories of the Canopy

In the canopy high, there's drama for show,
A squirrel's acrobatics, the stars of the show.
With a flip and a twirl, it leaps with a grin,
While birds cheer on, "You can't help but win!"

A wise old owl, with spectacles tight,
Tells tales of mischief, and the moon's flight.
A raccoon hears, with a paw on its chin,
"Who knew that tree-bark could taste like a win?"

Each branch holds stories, of days long ago,
Where the world was simpler, and time moved slow.
Giggling ferns join the laughing parade,
As the canopy sways, in twilight's charade.

When morning arrives, with laughter so sweet,
The animals gather, a joyous retreat.
In timeless stories, the fun never ends,
For in nature's arms, we're always friends.

The Island's Silent Embrace

On sandy shores where crabs all dance,
A coconut dreams of its big romance.
With seagulls squawking, a comedy show,
As sunscreen spills like a slippery flow.

The palm trees giggle, swaying with glee,
A llama in shorts? Now that's quite a spree!
As beach balls bounce with silly delight,
While fish trade gossip on the sea's left and right.

Sunbathers lounge like they're counting the sheep,
While jellyfish frolic in their gooey leap.
The island hums with a playful tune,
Where every sunset is a clumsy cartoon.

So let's toast to laughter on golden sands,
Where flip-flops fly in unruly bands.
Life's a beach joke, we all agree,
Let's ride the waves of pure jubilee!

Epiphanies in the Unseen

In shadows cast by a lazy sun,
A lone iguana thinks he's number one.
He struts and poses, with style so keen,
While the tourists chuckle, 'What a scene!'

Here, the coconuts laugh with a hearty thunk,
As squirrels hold meetings in the old tree trunk.
When sandcastles fall, it's quite the play,
As waves shout back, 'We're here to stay!'

The hidden wonders that tickle the mind,
Are the mischievous antics that nature designed.
A crab in a tux? Oh, what a sight!
He prances around, oh what pure delight!

On this island, laughs sprout all around,
With secret giggles in every sound.
Nature's own jokes bring joy ever seen,
In this quirky dance of the tropical green.

Canvas of a Tropical Dawn

At dawn's first light, the colors collide,
With flamingos wearing hues of pride.
A toucan crows with a beak so loud,
While crickets snicker amidst the crowd.

The sun stretches wide, yawning in glee,
As if it's saying, 'Look at me!'
The ocean chuckles, waves in a rush,
While dolphins tease with a cheeky hush.

Morning's a canvas with nature's brush,
Where bananas giggle in a fruity hush.
And parrots squawk tales of last night's feast,
About raccoons painting in the moonlight's east.

"Oh look!" says a starfish, "A shell I adore!"
While hermit crabs march with style to the shore.
A masterpiece crafted with smiles and cheer,
In this dawn, fun's the real souvenir!

Imprints of the Blushing Twilight

As twilight blushes with violet hue,
The island stirs, oh what a view!
Hermit crabs dance with pinch and prance,
While nocturnal critters join in the chance.

The moon winks down on a lazy cat,
As it ponders the merits of friendship with that.
Fireflies dazzle, having their ball,
As the stars play tag, oh they never fall!

With laughter hidden in the night air,
The gentle waves whisper secrets they share.
A turtle chuckles at the silly tide,
While geckos bond on their sticky slide.

So here's to the night, all wrinkled and bright,
With giggles echoing till the morning light.
In this twilight glow, joy finds its way,
Leaving imprints of fun till the break of day!

Guardians of the Tropical Shore

On the beach, the crabs do strut,
Wearing shells, they shake their butt.
Turtles nap, so wise and slow,
Laughter echoes, 'What a show!'

Seagulls swoop with comic flair,
Stealing fries without a care.
Coconuts drop with a thud,
Nature's prank—oh, what a dud!

The sun's a big, bright smiling face,
While waves dance with a funny grace.
Fishy jokes beneath the tide,
Whisper secrets, gills open wide.

With every breeze, a silly sigh,
As chubby dolphins leap and fly.
They spin and swirl like dancing fools,
Making waves—or breaking rules!

Echoes of the Warm Breeze

In the air, a tickling tease,
Whispers float on playful breeze.
A lizard yawns, and then he slips,
While nearby, a parrot flips!

Bananas laugh, they swing and sway,
As monkeys join the wild ballet.
Palm trees gossip, waving high,
"Did you see that? Oh my, my!"

Sandcastles rise, just to fall,
Shells giggle; it's a beachy brawl.
The sun's a joker, tossing rays,
While shadows play in funny ways.

And every wave that comes ashore,
Brings tales of laughter, never bore.
In this paradise, joy's abound,
With every silly sight and sound!

Melodies from a Leafy Oasis

In the shade, where laughter grows,
Frogs croak tunes, in wacky throes.
Leaves rustle like a band on cue,
While branches sway—oh, what a view!

A monkey strums an old guitar,
Notes float high, they go so far.
Chickens dance to each beat they make,
Shaking feathers; what a shake!

Mangoes tumble with a thud,
Juicy jokes, a fruity flood.
Caterpillars cha-cha by,
With silly steps, oh my, oh my!

In this haven, giggles reign,
Nature dances, but not in vain.
With melodies to lift the day,
It's a joyful, leafy play!

Visions Amidst the Verdant Silence

In leafy depths, the humor woke,
Where vines twist like an old joke.
A chipmunk wears a tiny hat,
And struts about—imagine that!

Sunlight tickles, shadows prance,
While flowers join in a silly dance.
A bear sneezes, oh what a sound,
Leaves flutter, laughter's all around!

Time flows slow in this green land,
With every critter playing grand.
A silly squirrel in a race,
Trips, but giggles light his face.

Under canopies, mischief brews,
Nature's jokes, it gladly woos.
In this quiet, fun's the way,
With every leaf, it finds a play!

Conversations with the Moonlit Trunks

Underneath the glow so bright,
The trees spoke secrets, what a sight!
One croaked jokes, the other laughed,
A leafy chat, their joy a craft.

They whispered tales of summer nights,
Of wiggly worms and slippery bites.
The breeze chimed in, a giggling sound,
A playful dance, they twirled around.

Moths joined in, with fluttery grace,
Joining the trees in this silly space.
"Why did the branch reach for the sky?"
"Because it wanted to be a high-flyer, oh my!"

Their laughter echoed, a sound so sweet,
A choir of nature, no need for a seat.
In this funny bough brigade, joy rings true,
As trunks chat freely under skies of blue.

Sighs in the Summer's Embrace

Sunshine hat perched on its head,
A tree sighed softly, feeling dread.
"Why can't I hop? I want to run!"
The roots just chuckled, "You're not that fun!"

The branches stretched, to tickle a cloud,
"Join us!" they beckoned, feeling proud.
But clouds just giggled, fluffy and white,
"We float around, it's our delight!"

And then came a breeze, twirling about,
"Let's race!" it shouted, full of clout.
The trees stood still, not one would budge,
"We'd rather stay here, no need to trudge!"

Yet through all the sighs and moments grim,
The trees shared laughter on a playful whim.
In the arms of summer, under skies of glee,
Laughter prevailed, as it always should be.

Shimmering Tales of the Tropics

In a land where coconuts sway,
The parrots burst in, bright and gay.
"Tell us a tale, oh wise old tree!"
"Can you make it fun? Let it be zany!"

The trunk scratched its bark, deep in thought,
"Once I had a fruit that really fought!
It rolled away, what a slippery deed,
Chased it down till I lost all my speed!"

The leaves erupted in fluttering cheer,
"Let's spread the word, let all creatures hear!"
The iguanas laughed, with a joyful cheer,
"Mirthful tales, oh come here, dear!"

From the lizards to the crabs on the sand,
All gathered 'round, in a humorous band.
In vibrant tropics, where stories unfold,
Laughter reigns true, and fun is gold.

Dreams Beneath a Velvet Sky

The stars blinked bright, winking with glee,
A dreaming tree sang, "Oh, listen to me!"
"Last night I danced, oh what a sight!
Pairing with shadows till the morning light!"

The moon chimed in, with a chuckle loud,
"Not half as good as the trees of the crowd!"
They swayed in rhythm, a whimsical trance,
All foliage ready for this starry dance.

With roots tapping softly on soft green ground,
They spun with joy, without a sound.
Yet the fireflies giggled, lighting the scene,
"Ballet in the breeze, oh it's so serene!"

So dreams intertwined 'neath the sky's embrace,
With twinkling giggles, they found their place.
In the dance of the night, with humor grand,
Nature's comedy, the best in the land.

www.ingramcontent.com/pod-product-compliance
Lightning Source LLC
Chambersburg PA
CBHW072134070526
44585CB00016B/1670